Black in White

Here is your heart

and other poems from the
Black in White Poetry Competition 2022

CHARLOTTE SHYLLON

+ 27 contributing poets

Second Edition

This book, originally titled Black in White Community Collection Volume 2, has been retitled Here is Your Heart. We have made this change for two key reasons:

- To acknowledge the first prize winner Rebecca Caine's poem from the Black in White Poetry Competition 2022.

- To ensure all of the books in the Black in White series have a clearly different identity, while remaining under the same umbrella brand.

We have also taken the opportunity to commission an illustration for the front cover from illustrator Tia Miles, of Tia Diana Draws, to reflect the title and contents of Serena's poem.

We hope you like this book's new identity and enjoy reading this powerful collection of poems by 28 poets!

CONTENTS

Section 5:
About Black in White ... 101

Dedication

This book, like its predecessor, is dedicated to all those who see and value the benefits of equality, diversity and inclusion, and who labour actively in whatever capacity within this field to help open the minds of those who are the reason why these poems have been written…

Acknowledgements

I would like to acknowledge several people who have been instrumental in helping me to compile the contents for this book.

☺ All the poetry competition entrants, especially those featured in this book. Without their poems, this book wouldn't be as content rich as it is. Not everyone could be selected and celebrated publicly, but I appreciate everyone's efforts.

☺ My fellow judges in the second Black in White Poetry Competition – Avril Lee, Marcia McKnight and Serena Malcolm – who diligently undertook an iterative judging process to select the winning and highly commended poems.

☺ The members of the Black in White team – my sisters Hanna and Deborah, Marcia McKnight, Sarah Murray, Denyse Barwick and David Balfour – who give many hours to our common passion project.

☺ All my other family and friends who gave an encouraging word or two along the way.

☺ My children, Andrew and Olivia Coker, who share their mother with her laptop on all those mornings, nights and weekends when I work on Black in White activities.

☺ Most of all, I thank God for giving me the strength and focus to continue on this journey.

FOREWORD

Dear Reader

I have just watched the Queen's funeral and find myself thinking about how Britain has changed, seen in the faces of the queue who filed silently past and in the armed forces personnel and crowds that gathered today. Our history too was clearly in view; outstanding achievements, but also shared pain and colonial times, reflected by the dignitaries attending the ceremony and those in the procession. The Queen oversaw the birth of a modern, more diverse nation – and many of our own families and friends are a product of that. I, as an Irish Hong Konger of British birth, feel this very strongly.

But the creation of modern Britain, official and personal, was often difficult and challenging. The poems in this competition speak to this shared history and the evolution to become a modern community formed by people from many places. Poetry of lived experience, poetry of how history shaped us, poetry of pain, rejection, and hate, but also poetry of positive bonding, poetry of the energy created by new communities, and poetry of humanity over power.

The power of poetry is distinct. It distils emotions and conveys experiences better than any other creative art. As I read the poems I was moved, more than I ever expected, and then made angry, disgusted and frustrated that individuals are still being denied fair opportunities, are attacked and made to feel less, to be devalued. I was also inspired and felt the beauty of the poems; as well as recognising parts of my life and those of my family.

I want to say a personal thank you to Charlotte for establishing such a powerful platform to hear ordinary voices, to register the injustice of racism and call for true inclusiveness. Charlotte herself is a unique individual, combining a successful communications career with being a poet alongside a commitment to driving change for people of colour.

I know you will find all the poems in this remarkable book equally moving and uplifting and I want to thank all who shared their experiences and creativity to enter the competition. For those who won, congratulations, and for those who didn't, we heard your voice. This book represents global Britain, a world of change and many lives lived. And in this week of Britain in the spotlight, we remember Chris Kaba – and recognise another family facing an unacceptable loss. Just as we call to remember him and #Sayhisname, we acknowledge the power of the word.

Avril Lee
Head of Healthcare Europe, Zeno Group and Chair of the Chartered Institute of Public Relations' Diversity and Inclusion Network

INTRODUCTION

Why we must continue to share our stories about racism

The journey continues

The journey I began two years ago continues. This is the third book I have released under the Black in White umbrella to share stories about the racism black people encounter every day.

I was compelled to take action after the horrific murder of George Floyd. This tragic event woke the world up to the deadly consequences that can occur when racism is out of control. A policeman in Minneapolis, USA, who had pledged to 'serve and protect' took the life of a man *suspected* of a crime because he couldn't see beyond his victim's black skin.

Yet as I write these words, two years on from George's killing, here in the UK we're waiting to find out why Chris Kaba – another unarmed black man – had his life cut short when he was shot and fatally injured by a firearms police officer. From what I understand using lethal or deadly force is "justified only under conditions of extreme necessity as a last resort, when all lesser means have failed or cannot reasonably be employed". It remains to be seen whether that was the case with 24-year-old Chris.

Sad to say, George and Chris are not alone. In May 2021, *Newsweek* reported that at least 229 black people had been killed by the police in America one year on from George Floyd's killing. Proportionally, this was the same as in previous years. Nothing changed. In fact, according to an article on *NBC News* in March 2022, things got worse. They reported that the number of black people killed by police had actually increased over the last two years, and that black people remain twice as likely as white people to be shot and killed by police officers.

The disproportionate killing of black people by the police is not only an issue in the USA. According to an independent review of deaths in police custody in the UK, between 1990 and 2009, 16% of those who died after the use of force were black — more than twice the proportion arrested.

What has all of this got to do with racism in the workplace, you may ask. Well what happens in society impacts and influences thinking and behaviours in every part of our lives, and our workplaces are a microcosm of society. So the journey continues…

Make no room for diversity fatigue

Diversity fatigue wasn't a term I was familiar with until about 18 months ago. As I learned more about it, I came to understand that it's become a bit of a blanket term used to describe a variety of situations. According to *chieflearningofficer.com*, these include "resistance against political correctness", feeling overwhelmed by the amount of diversity work still required, and disappointment in the "all talk, no action" phenomenon.

I take serious issue with those who are feeling diversity fatigue that's based on resistance to political correctness. We need to make no room for those who say they're tired of hearing about the need for diversity, and all the accompanying factors including equity, equality, inclusion and belonging. As I explain in one of my new poems, *Diversity Fatigue? I'm Tired Too…*, those of us impacted by racism can't escape it. It finds us even if we try to avoid it. Imagine how tired — nay, exhausted — black people are of this!

In my opinion, diversity fatigue in this context is just another way of saying black people are playing the race card. It's designed to switch off black voices. But we need to keep speaking up — to be the squeaky wheel — continuing to draw attention to the issue of racism. That's the only way we will either guilt or educate people into taking action against it.

Education is key. We can't just leave those who express or exhibit that they are experiencing diversity fatigue to continue in their ignorance. Their perspectives need to be listened to, so we can understand and address their issues appropriately. My point is this… everyone's voice is important, and every voice needs to be heard. After all, that's what diversity is about. However, diversity fatigue views that seek to extinguish the flame of change should not be accommodated. Employees need to be provided with access and pointed to the right resources so they can educate themselves and try to understand the value of actively eliciting, embracing and embedding perspectives that are different to their own.

For those feeling overwhelmed by how much work still needs to be done around diversity, I empathise – but we need to be indefatigable. As the statistics I quoted earlier attest, real change doesn't happen overnight (even after a seismic event like George Floyd's murder!). Nevertheless, if we simply allow the task at hand to overwhelm us, the already slim chance of any meaningful change will at best plateau. Diversity fatigue should never be accepted as a reason, or used as an excuse, for not continuing to pursue and implement diversity initiatives. Those charged with this responsibility, need to have effective strategies in place to combat diversity fatigue should it arise.

While progress on several diversity fronts is slow, one positive outcome of the Black Lives Matter movement in the UK over the last two years is that an increasing number of companies are talking about diversity and its benefits. That's great. There are, of course, the "all talk, no action brigade" who are only concerned with the optics. This type of lip service to diversity can be disappointing, demoralising and demotivating. We need to challenge this approach wherever possible.

For the companies who are not just talking but are taking action to embed diversity in their organisations, action in itself isn't the end goal – it must lead to measurably better outcomes. This can only be achieved if employers have robust diversity strategies in place and hold themselves accountable for meeting clearly stated key performance indicators. It's about progress, not intention. As the management guru Peter Drucker said, "What gets measured gets done". Activity for activity's sake is just activity.

Racism doesn't just happen at work

So far, I've focused on racism in the police force and in workplaces, but there is another area that greatly concerns me – and that's the issue of racism in childhood. This was brought sharply into focus this year when the story about Child Q broke. She is a teenager who was subjected to degrading, disgusting and discriminatory maltreatment that has had a hugely damaging effect on her. Suspected by her teachers of having used cannabis, she was taken out of an exam at school and subjected by two female police officers to an invasive strip search in the school's medical room while on her period. A safeguarding review concluded that "racism (whether deliberate or not) was likely to have been an influencing factor in the decision to undertake a strip search".

As the mother of a black teenage girl myself, the story of Child Q breaks my heart. My Olivia could have been Child Q; like Child Q, she was 15 years old in 2020. The thought that she could have been wrongly targeted by racist police officers is anathema to me.

The Metropolitan Police said the incident was "regrettable" and "should never have happened". But it did. It's not the first time an innocent black child has encountered racism at the hands of the police and, sadly, it won't be the last time either. Diane Abbot, the MP for Hackney North and Stoke Newington where Child Q's school is located, confirmed that of the 25 strip searches of under-18s in the borough in 2020-21, 23 were black children.

Those of us who parent black children are all too familiar with the stories they tell us and our own responses of the racism, microaggressions and unconscious bias that they encounter in schools. Take, for example, the below extract from an email I sent to my son's school in 2017:

"I understand from my son that a pupil has made some racist and severely violent threats against him and other ethnic minority students. I must admit I am surprised that the school did not to make the parents of the boys who have been threatened aware of this. I understand that the school has involved the police and imposed some sanctions against the boy, but that he is back at school – and the boys he racially abused were told that 'he needs support'. That's all very well and good, but more importantly – is the boy receiving instruction on why his views are wrong? … Has the school considered that the students who were subject to his threats may also need support?"

The school was very careful not to respond in writing. I received a phone call from one of the senior staff who essentially told me that they couldn't talk to me for confidentiality reasons, a lame excuse that failed to address my very real concerns. The boy remained in school, seemingly having "got away with it", sending a message to those he'd threatened that they were less valued.

Racism is real and it's institutionalised – schools are no exception. Racism, wherever it occurs, is based on ignorant views that are entrenched and persistent. We need to call out racism whenever it occurs. We must work towards becoming an anti-racist society.

Poems about experiences of childhood racism

That's why, this year we extended the Black in White Poetry Competition to include childhood racism as a second category, so we could air some of these stories.

All of the entries we received to the poetry competition were excellent, across the board. However, and perhaps unsurprisingly, all of the winning poems this year make mention to a greater or lesser degree of childhood experiences of racism. Whether written by adults relating long-past incidents that impacted their lives then, and in many cases continue to impact them now, or by children relating more recent experiences of racism, the other judges and I were moved and mortified by their accounts in equal proportions. These poems powerfully demonstrate the discrimination and marginalisation that black children experience and put a human face to racism in a way that statistics alone can't.

Workplace racism continues to be a key area of focus for us at Black in White. Many of the highly commended poems exemplify this issue. Furthermore, of the six poems I penned for this book, three are in the workplace category, two straddle both categories, and one is in the childhood category.

We will retain the childhood category in our poetry competitions, alongside the workplace category, going forward. From next year, however, we will judge each category separately and award separate winners' prizes per category. Watch this space.

Racism is all around us and stories like the ones featured in this book need to be told. That's why our mission at Black in White – to contribute through poetry to the conversation about ending racism – must, and will, continue.

Charlotte Shyllon
Founder and Chief Creative Officer, Black in White

SECTION 1:

About the Black in White Poetry Competition 2022

Black in White
Poetry
Competition
2022
Have you experienced racism, prejudice, unconscious bias or microaggressions as a child or as a working adult?
We are launching our second poetry competition, and are calling on you to write about experiences of racism – either yours or someone else's, and either in the workplace or in your childhood – and to share the impact these experiences have had on your life.

Black in White Poetry Competition 2022

After the release of my first book of poems, *Black in White*, in November 2020 and its official launch in May 2021, I decided to run a poetry competition to give other people an opportunity to air some of their experiences of racism in their own voices. The first Black in White Poetry Competition was open for entries for about seven weeks in Summer 2021. With my three co-judges, we selected our three winners and 25 highly commended entries.

We announced the results on our website and social media channels in September and two months later, in November, launched an anthology titled *Black in White Community Collection*. This comprised the 28 selected entries as well as several poems written by five guest poets and me.

Even back then, I'd said that we would run a bigger and better competition in 2022 – and we have. We extended the entry categories to two, calling not just for experiences of racism in the workplace but also in childhood. We also launched this book one month earlier than last year, during the UK's Black History Month celebration in October.

We brought new judges on board, including the first prize winner of our 2021 competition, Serena Malcolm, and two communications professionals, Avril Lee and Marcia McKnight – their biographies follow towards the end of this section. Unfortunately, three other judges were unable, ultimately, to participate in the process for various reasons, but I thank them for their engagement and encouragement.

As in 2021, this year we followed a rigorous judging process. The judges reviewed all the entries anonymously, giving equal value to all poems in both categories including those from overseas; we received entries not just from the UK, but from other countries such as the USA, Germany and India. Judging involved a detailed initial sift of the almost 80 shortlisted poems we received followed by first round scoring of the poems by each of the judges individually against six criteria: beauty, power, education or entertainment; technical excellence; form and flow; choice of words and readability; overall impact; and polish and expertise.

The scores were summarised, and poems were listed in order based on the total scores they received. The judges then reviewed and discussed this allocation to ensure that we were happy with the winning and highly commended selections and that all the poems exemplified the competition's objectives.

This year, we awarded four main prizes; after choosing the 1st and 2nd place prizes winners, we ended up selecting two 3rd place prize winners since the judges felt that both of their poems warranted the position. The 1st prize winner this year was Rebecca Caine with her poem *Here is Your Heart*, an evocative and emotional reflection on the power and influence of a father's heart on his daughter through his experiences of racism and by the example he set her. The second prize winner was Aretha Ahunanya with *Monotypic Blackness*. This poem provides a powerful perspective through the eyes of young black girl who refuses to be defined by her colour.

The third prize places were awarded to Mervyn Seivwright with *A Boy Created a Noose at Eight*, a hard-hitting tale of the sometimes tragic consequences of racism in childhood and Samiya Hamid with *'A Normal Day'* where we experience a young boy's introduction to racism juxtaposed with his mother's acceptance of his eye-opening experience as normality. We also doubled the value of the third prize. We awarded 27 poems as highly commended. Interestingly this year we received multiple entries from several entrants; each were reviewed anonymously, and consequently five authors have two poems each in this book.

The poetry competition has now become an annual fixture on the Black in White calendar, and will be run again in 2023, so look out for the launch announcements in due course.

Charlotte Shyllon

Judges Biographies

❖ **Avril Lee** is a communications practitioner who, as Head of Healthcare Europe at Zeno Group, specialises in healthcare campaigns working alongside patient groups, healthcare professionals and health companies internationally and in the UK. She chairs the Chartered Institute of Public Relations' Diversity and Inclusion Network and is a Trustee of Doctors of the World UK, a charity that campaigns for access to health for disenfranchised communities.

❖ **Marcia McKnight** has a 30-year public relations and marketing communications career in the NHS, local government and charity sectors. Marcia was the first black director of communications in a NHS Trust. She is a qualified nurse, former chair of school governors and victim support volunteer. She is also a member of the Black in White team.

❖ **Serena Malcolm** is an ex-police officer who has been writing poetry for over 3 decades. She draws influence from her time in the force, her work in youth and mental health services, and her experiences as a woman of mixed heritage growing up in London. She currently works for a local authority. Her poem *'Foreign Body'* won the 2021 Black in White Poetry Competition.

Judge's Commentary

I have been writing poetry for over three decades, but I have only recently begun to share my work. Having grown up as a dual-heritage child in London, and having worked as a police officer in one of the most diverse cities in the world, I am certainly no stranger to racism; both in childhood, and the workplace. So, in 2021, when I happened upon a flyer for the first Black in White Poetry Competition, I immediately fell in love with the premise. I submitted three of my poems, but I submitted them with absolutely no expectations. I wanted to win, of course, but I was so unsure of myself that I had already made peace with the possibility of not even placing. I submitted my entries and promptly put the competition out of my mind.

As you can imagine, receiving the news several weeks later that I had won the first-place prize completely blew me away. It was at that point that I realised just how much I really had wanted to win. It was a victory not only in terms of the competition, but also a personal victory; I had put my work out there for the first time and I felt like I had truly been seen. I had been validated. This feeling was further galvanised when I attended the book launch and got to hear, and later read, some of the other entries. The calibre was impressive, the content; inspiring. And reciting my poem in front of everyone in attendance – another first for me – was fulfilling in a way I cannot describe.

The whole experience is one that I will remember forever. When I was asked to be a judge for the 2022 competition, I was truly honoured. There was absolutely no hesitation on my part when it came to accepting. It had been such a wonderful experience the year before that I felt grateful to be a part of it a second time.

I was so genuinely impressed by the quality of entries. Impressed, too, by the diversity of voice, style, and lived experience. There was an abundance of passion, mainly, I believe, due to the addition of the 'childhood racism' category. The entries to this category in particular were evocative and profound. Their stories were real, their pain almost palpable.

I think all of the judges would agree that choosing a winner was no mean feat. I can honestly say that there were no poems that did not belong. However, when we came together to make that final decision, the vibrancy of debate sparked by some of the entries steered us towards on our deserving winners. To all of this year's entrants I would like to say, from one poet to another, that you should be so very proud. The difficulty we had in making our selection is a testament to your talent. And to all future entrants – especially those as unsure as I was – I say, go for it, put yourself out there, take that chance.

You are good enough.

Serena Malcolm

SECTION 2:

Poems by Charlotte Shyllon

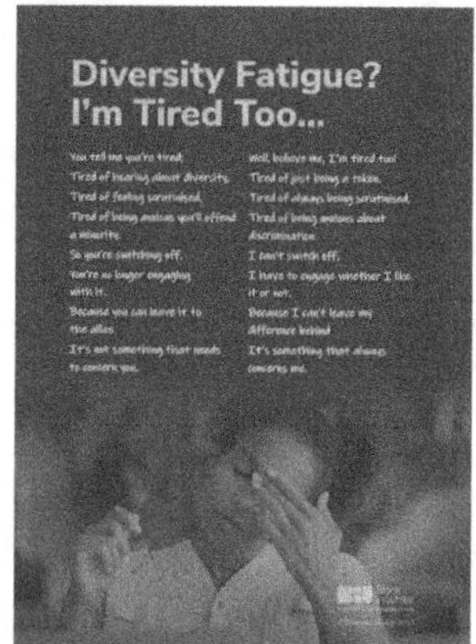

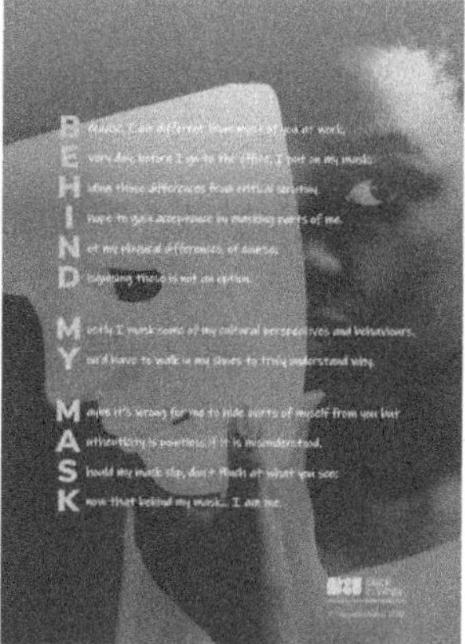

These poems are available to purchase as individual postcards and posters (priced from £2.50 to £8.50 + postage & packaging) from

www.blackinwhiteservices.co.uk.

I have written six new poems for this book. The inspiration and context for each poem is below:

- ❖ **BELONGING:** Abraham Maslow's hierarchy of needs pyramid places belonging as the third in a five-step process that leads to true fulfilment. Today many equality, diversity and inclusion and employee engagement experts recognise that true traction cannot be achieved in their organisations without belonging. When employees feel that they truly belong at work, they feel more connected and committed. This poem champions the need for belonging to help ensure that we can all achieve our best.

- ❖ **BEING BLACK BRITISH:** I'm frequently struck by the fact that even though so many black people were born here and have lived here all of their lives, some white people never accept them as British. Yet go back a few generations, and some of the people who view black people as 'foreigners' might actually be from foreign stock themselves. They've just been able to blend in because of their white skin – and recent European migrants enjoy the same privilege. Three times, this poem asks the question, 'What does being black British mean?' and provides some responses. It ends with a positive call to action.

- ❖ **BLACK IN WHITE:** This short shape poem makes a simple point. The point being that while there are challenges to being a minority when some of those in the majority see you as less, you must continue to have hope for a future that will allow you truly to be free.

- ❖ **DIVERSITY FATIGUE? I'M TIRED TOO…:** When I first heard the term diversity fatigue I was disappointed. Some people are actually tired of hearing about diversity and inclusion? Black people have been facing racism for far longer than anyone has been talking about why things needs to change. Imagine how tired we are! This poem compares and contrasts both perspectives.

- ❖ **SHOCKED INTO SILENCE NO MORE:** This poem starts by describing two encounters I had several decades ago, one in school and one at university, that happened because of ignorance about black people. It relates the impact these had on me – making me keep silent about my African roots in certain circles because I thought that would help me to fit in. That all changed when George Floyd was murdered…

- ❖ **HISTORY IS NOT MY STORY:** Children are not born racist; they learn racism through what they are taught and what they observe. Similarly, children can't become what they can't see. So we need to change the narrative around the black history that is taught in schools to change children's learned racial perspectives from negative to positive.

Quotable Quotes

If we cannot now end our differences, at least we can help make the world safe for diversity.

John F. Kennedy

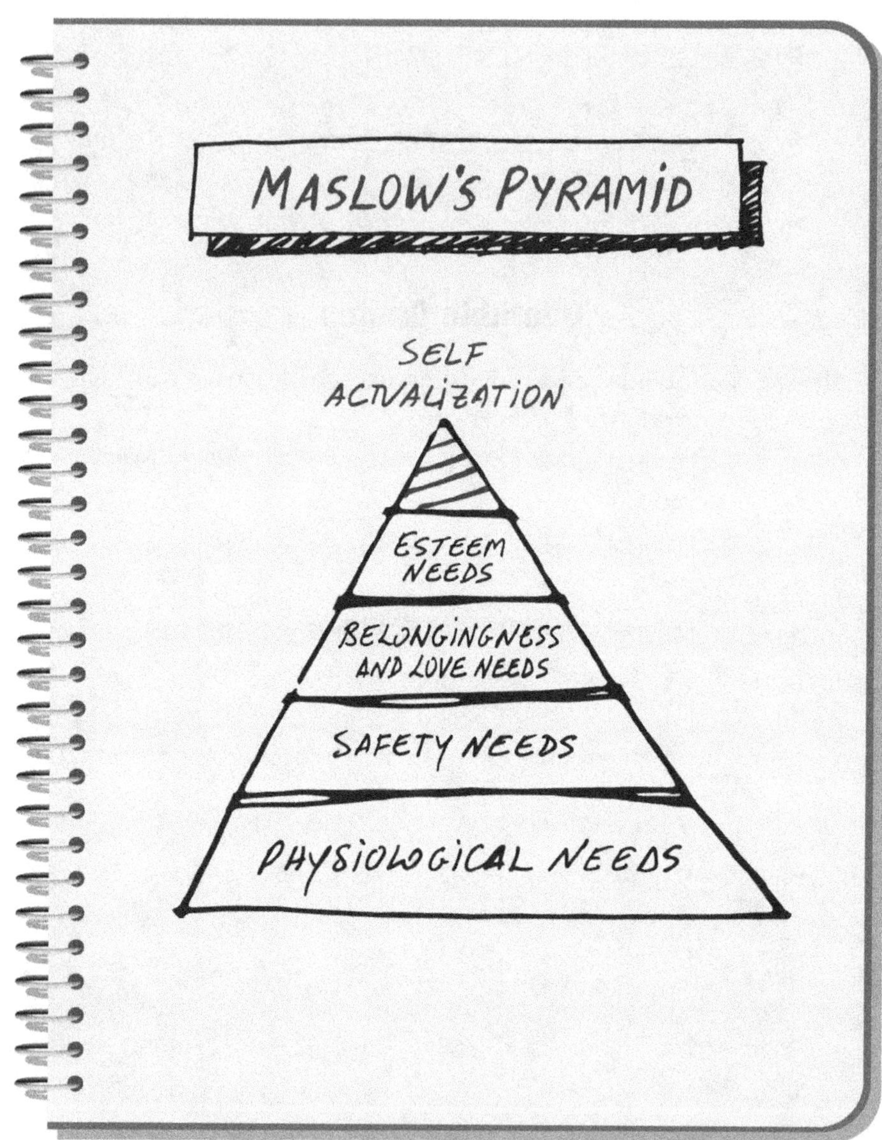

MASLOW'S PYRAMID
SELF ACTUALIZATION
ESTEEM NEEDS
BELONGINGNESS AND LOVE NEEDS
SAFETY NEEDS
PHYSIOLOGICAL NEEDS

BELONGING

Maslow was correct…
He said we need to connect.
He said without belonging
We will always be longing
For those higher tiers.
But for all to climb the stairs
That lead to esteem,
And take us upstream
To self-actualisation,
We must embrace the realisation
That diversity and inclusion
Isn't an optical illusion.
It's about creating real change
So we can broaden the range.
Value everyone the same
So we can all win the game.
With no unfair block or stop
We could all reach the top.

BEING BLACK BRITISH

What does being black British mean?
It means always being seen.
It means being different from the masses
Unlike a foreigner who passes,
Who quickly blends in
Because of their white skin.
But black natives stick out
And so get kicked about.

What does being black British mean?
It means even when you're a teen
You may be treated with disdain.
You may struggle to retain
A positive outlook on your life
When your face may bring strife,
When you may be hated
Instead of celebrated.

What does being black British mean?
It means you have to be keen,
Much keener than the rest
To achieve your best.
It means needing a strong self-belief
Winning in ways that bring relief.
So don't give up or resort to crying,
Believe in yourself and keep on trying!

BLACK IN WHITE

I
am
black
in white,
often held back,
often have to fight
not to be viewed as less,
often it's hard, I must confess
to remain positive when people mess.
Though it may be hard to conceive,
I choose to hope and believe,
that I will truly perceive
a much better way
for us all one day,
then I can be
truly free
to be
me.

DIVERSITY FATIGUE? I'M TIRED TOO...

You tell me you're tired;
Tired of hearing about diversity,
Tired of feeling scrutinised,
Tired of being anxious you'll offend a minority.
So you're switching off,
You're no longer engaging with it.
Because you can leave it to the allies
It's not something that needs to concern you.

Well, believe me, I'm tired too!
Tired of just being a token,
Tired of always being scrutinised,
Tired of being anxious about discrimination.
I can't switch off,
I have to engage whether I like it or not.
Because I can't leave my difference behind
It's something that always concerns me.

SHOCKED INTO SILENCE NO MORE

In the mid-70s as a young teen
Fresh from Africa, new on the scene,
I was shocked when school mates cornered me
To ask if back home I'd slept in a tree!
They thought all Africans were really poor
And that lions and elephants lived next door.
Asked if my colour would change if I showered
I said no politely, but inwardly cowered.

These were girls at a private school
Who I'd thought would be really cool.
Shocked into silence, I didn't say much
My African identity kept to light touch.
I chose to retreat into my shell
Because being different felt like hell;
The few girls I let in were welcoming and nice
But I had to pretend I preferred chips to rice!

Then in the 80s at university
A friend I'd made from a Northern city
Wanted to go to London with me
To party and meet my family.
But a few days later she said she couldn't go.
The reason why? Because she didn't know
How she'd cope around so many black folk!
I was so hurt, my spirit broke.

The impact of those shocks from my younger days
Made me tread carefully in so many ways;
From then, I was careful when choosing my friends
To avoid relationships with twists and bends.
To some I seemed quiet, too reserved
But that reputation was undeserved;
It wasn't so much that I was shrinking
More like "strategic overthinking".

At work I learned to play the game,
Kept my head down and was pretty tame.
My approach worked in part – I got promoted
But the impact on my soul can't be sugar-coated.
I never really felt free to be me,
I masked parts I didn't want colleagues to see;
I couldn't be authentic in a workplace
Where I could be judged on my face or race.

It took another shock to open my eyes.
The murder of George Floyd made me realise
If I just stayed silent nothing could change;
I had to speak up, even if it felt strange.
Will speaking up make a real impact?
It's hard to be sure, that's a fact.
But one thing that's abundantly clear to me
Is that by speaking out, I can set myself free.

Quotable Quotes

When you hear people making hateful comments, stand up to them. Point out what a waste it is to hate, and you could open their eyes.

Taylor Swift

HISTORY IS NOT MY STORY

The black history we're taught in school
Is really uncool.
It's a carefully crafted narrative
That's horribly reductive.
It's not our true story,
It focuses on the gory.
Like the scenes we see on TV
Of African poverty,
That show just one perspective,
That's not wholly representative.
Like films showing old colonial masters
Ruling black nations like new massas.

But black history is more than slavery,
There are lots of stories of our bravery.
There's much in our past to celebrate.
Black heroes we should venerate.
Teach children how we fought in world wars,
Helped keep the enemies from our doors.
Tell them we didn't just arrive on a boat;
We were invited to help keep Britain afloat.
Even as far back as Medieval days
We helped to shape the British ways.
Correct the prequel, to secure the sequel.
Let children know that we're all equal.

SECTION 3:

Poetry Competition 2022:
Winning Poems

HERE IS YOUR HEART

By Rebecca Caine

Yesterday morning, with nothing to do
I turned on the radio.
Black people are nine times more likely to be
stopped and searched, I heard a presenter say.
I was sent into the past –

A past where from out my window,
I saw a policeman stop my Dad on our drive,
I saw my Dad pull out his ID, nod his head
and wait.
The policeman left, my Dad closed our gate.

My Dad gave me life
Here is your body, your soul, your heart
Here are your gifts, your love, your strife
Here is your youth, your black joy, your art

A past where I heard my Mum say,
Dad's been passed over at work.
A white less qualified man got the promotion,
all I knew was my Dad was sad.
Was it workplace discrimination or nothing personal?

My Dad gave me wisdom
Here is your judgment, your intellect, your why
Here is your walk, your dance, your beat of drum
Here is your gut, your fairness, your rights

A past where I was walking with my Dad in town.
A man stared at us with a smirk
and then whispered a slur.
My Dad walked past saying that was not right,
he was full of anger that night.
My Dad gave me a beating heart
Here is your black honour, your pride, your courage
Here are your kings: Marcus Garvey, Alf Valentine, Samuel Sharpe
Here's how to eat ripe mango, sip your Wray & Nephew,
jerk your pork

Now back in the present, I can't ask my Dad as he's no longer here –
how much racism, how did you keep your faith?
But I have the gift of his roots,
roots that grow deep and strong
roots that own his power and belong.

Quotable Quotes

It is not our differences that divide us. It is our inability to recognise, accept, and celebrate those differences.

Audre Lorde

MONOTYPIC BLACKNESS

By Aretha Ahunanya

I am black.

But what does that mean?

You see, I can only show you this from my perspective
Can't define or generalise the whole collective
That's the truth.
Because black is not confined to one shade of skin
It's culture, it's history
Ingrained within
My family, My ancestry
Everything.

For my mum –
Emigrating here aged 18
Or my dad –
Born and raised in Hackney, East.

They made sure I knew where I was from
The lengths they'd gone
To make sure my brother and I
That we could thrive
So how dare you ever say
"I'm not black enough"?
"I talk white".
(Now that's another story altogether…)

The girls at school must think I'm a trend
Popular at one point, ignored the next.
The hair, the clothes, yeah that's cool
But not too much
Too "ratchet" – you'll look like a fool.

Mocking our names
From Oluwa to Babatunde, to them it's all the same
And the day I wear my hair in braids, it's –
"Oh!"
"I didn't recognise you."
"You look just like…"

that other black girl.

Some people want to be black
But just for a day.
When it comes to injustice, they all shy away
"Don't make it about race", they say
"We're all the same"

"Why make it something bigger?"
"Come on, it's just a song, so I can say 'nigger'" –
No you can't.

No
You can't.

And yet
I don't let that undermine me
I make the choice to use my voice
In a world that doesn't want to hear my noise.
A world all too willing for me to
Slip
Through
The cracks.
But I know
That I can't fit inside the lines
Trapped, confined
To whatever you define
as "black".

Quotable Quotes

We know that diversity can sometimes be more uncomfortable because things are less familiar – but it gets the best results.

Megan Smith

A BOY CREATED A NOOSE AT EIGHT

By Mervyn Seivwright

Gabriel,

was tormented,

a gentle lamb

herded by wolves

loved to look smart

incited a foretold necktie

he was on camera

circled

standing his ground

quickly slammed

the camera filming him

unconscious

lens focused for world view

no teachers to cease

four minutes

harassing the Raggedy Andy doll

still,

shoes kicking him, hands shoving

face

– making children laugh

at Carson Elementary School,

Principal shared a sequence

speaking to loving parents

hiding the truth

their son fainted asleep

from a bullied blackout,

descending off his bunkbed

on the third day.

A 'NORMAL' DAY

By Samiya Hamid

Just another normal day.
Yesterday morning, with nothing to do
A normal day you tell yourself,
Out with your mum,
11-years-old looking out for some fun,
Just finished primary school and thought you were done,
Until you look up from the floor and felt stunned.

You've met with the face of a familiar boy,
A boy from your class with a face full of joy,
Little did you know his smiles just a ploy
And his real intention was purely to destroy.

Naïve and innocent, you muster a "hello",
As he cycles around you in slow mo(tion),
Your mind flashes back to a moment ago,
Back into year six before the change began to forego.

He signed your yearbook with a sly little winky face,
Little did you know that little boy had been replaced,
His new mates circle round you making cruel comments on your race,
And the only emotion you feel in the moment is disgrace.

Confused and frightened, you look around,
Adults walk around as if they didn't hear a sound,
It's only in that moment you realise you are bound
Purely 'cuz they couldn't accept the fact that you are brown.

Besides you, mum's face looks in dismay,
She didn't want to teach you racism this way,
She glances to your distraught face and says 'block them away'
Then acts as if it was 'just another normal day'.

SECTION 4:

Poetry Competition 2022:
Highly Commended Poems

(in alphabetical order by poem title)

A GAME OF COLOUR

By Nofia Rochmond

They say I'm Indian,
Against the Palestinians,
A curry lover,
A terrorist undercover,
Brown in colour.

Do I reek that much?
Of my Biryani for lunch,
With hair like tendrils of a creeper,
A dirty, prejudiced against creature,
My face of grotesque features.

 Then in September was 911,
The start of weird looks and expressions,
My bag stared at like a dangerous weapon,
Am I a Sikh or Muslim they question?
I'm a Christian, a Hindu reflection.

But our culture is traditional and divine,
The Sari is out beauty and pride,
Now the West enjoy our food,
The delicacies delightfully chewed,
Our dance and singing pursued.

So we are more than just a race,
But a heritage to be embraced,
So don't hide in humiliation,
Freely express your culture without hesitation,
As we finally put an end to discrimination.

A HISTORY OF HYPOCRISY

By Lewis Searle

I sit in my history class, learning of inequality...
How Black people were treated in what they called democracy...
And, in my head, I picture myself in a courtroom,
Ready to explode... tick... tick... tick... BOOM!

I say,

"What's the point in courts of law if not to achieve justice?
You speak of the Constitution, but how am I supposed to trust this?
It was written by people just like you so God-damn hypocritical!
Owning slaves yet still claiming that all men are made up equal!
Oh well, guess Tom forgot to say 'bout the colour of their skin,
Gimme his Declaration and I'll throw it in the bin!
Let's turn quotas into quotes and treat them like the rest of us!
No more sitting in different places up and down and up and down the bus!

Why should colour matter anyway? Is that such a hard question?
You've answered many times and what's your best one?
Your logic's as flawed as your precious second amendment,
Now it's time for me to introduce my defendant!

Will this be a fair trial? Probably not,
To this day 'if you're Black you're six times more likely shot...

Newsflash America: Our great nation's
Built on racist foundations
And has a population
In need legal liberation!

Go on, ignore this, just like you've done for years,
I'm talking to you: supposed jury of my peers!"

AFTERBIRTH

By Mervyn Seivwright

We are not born to be martyrs
    before adulthood. Joan of Arc,
the warrior, was larger than her-
    self, Maid of Lorraine laid to rest
at nineteen, a country's desire
    for unity. Black children now
no longer watching fireworks,
    they are dispersed in explosive

manners, cocoons dried, joeys ripped
    from pockets, tulip bulbs burned
before blossom. They are not born
    to be martyrs before adulthood.
Judge Dredd firing two to the chest,
    one to the head, center mass groupings
to bleed out children: on a playground
    with play-gun, walking on the street,

ricocheted shell to car passenger,
    driver stopped in a car, at home
on a carport defending themselves,
    running in an alley—surrendering
with arms raised, existing. They are
    not born to be martyrs before
adulthood. These children, no longer
    cute teddies, bunnies, tall enough

to be threatening, made invisible,
    why—visible now when names
are echoed, their pictures on signs
    sung by street voices reverberating
those with no birth contract seeking
    inspirational exit. No
sequoia tree is old enough
    to produce paper for the list

of names in American's past century,
    to remember they are born to live.

BLACK SILENCE

By Ogochukwu Madu

Silent is the girl who learns that her colour is a bullseye for the boys with cheap jokes and quick quips.

Silent is she who learns the discomfort of her colour so she will draw a line across her lips and smile, becoming a caricature of her own character.

Silence is her shield, but it brings no bullets, only the taut skin stretched across her back, marred with the shrapnel of their words.

Her silence is power, she thinks. It erases their judgement, their looks, their contempt.

Her silence is power. But it is erasing her.

COURT

By Theresa Georges

Stepped up in the Employment Tribunal, 2018, Fitzalan Place
We've all been waiting, here it is, the start of my Case
I was so so nervous, it was written all over my Face
I was forced to endure this, and take it right back to Base.

Prepared as I could be and knowing the importance of my Representation,
Ready for the heat and here for the Tension.

Because it was deep and disturbing and based on Race
What they did to me, I can still feel a Trace
So much pressure, sitting stony Faced
I felt so out of my comfort zone like I was floating in Space.

I wasn't prepared, I had never done this Before
Standing up in the courtroom and taking on the Law
I had to do this, because what they did cut me Raw
And I would never want anyone to witness what I saw.

Shortly after we were all sworn in,
That's when the 3 Judges all walked in
My heart steady beating, my head gave a Spin
I felt very intimidated, but still lifted my Chin.

The accused looked like Vampire's sat in the back Row
I took a deep breath, kissed my ring said here we Go.

Sat up in Court Suited and Booted
But deep down inside I felt my heart had been Looted.

All the way through their Barrister looked me in my Eyes
We had several moments and I felt he was on my Side
I focused my mind, as I knew we were in for a long Ride,
After they denied they were wrong which was the biggest shock
and Suprise
Even their own Barrister looked Defied
They acted so dumb and told major Lies
Whilst sitting there smirking, but couldn't look me in the Eyes
But their shameful excuses the judges Denied
And I knew I had won as the Lord was my Guide.

Back then, I was unaware of the term 'Litigant in Person'
It's when you defend yourself in court with no Legal Representation
They racially harassed me in work, did I forget to mention?

Then made me feel Tension, like I deserved after school
Detention.

Impending Racism, Impending Doom
I was the only person of colour sat in the Room
Equality and diversity training? What a Joke!
They took it as their opportunity to shout out the N-word! I
actually Choked
My voice dry and husky, couldn't even manage a Croak
I vacated to the exit after grabbing my Coat

But I knew that I was harbouring the Truth
And when it was exposed this case would hit the Roof
I Tried to contact witnesses who saw it all, and were my Proof
I tracked them down with skills like a Sleuth
This case wasn't a dream, it wasn't a Spoof
But to save their jobs they denied the Truth.

Then one afternoon I was taking a Snooze
The press knocked on my door, I was national News.

Harassment, Entrapment
Up in court I gave the truthful Enactment.

DARTS

By Chan's Crown

I always felt famous parading Sainsbury's Isles with the security
behind me.
It gave me the knowledge that all I have to do is be black,
for anyone to be all up under my skin
because it's easy to project the hate you have within.

The word 'suspicious' tastes so sweet in your mouth, yet you don't know
about candy,
but you'll do the electric Slide when a hooded black boy walks by,
because you want to safeguard your purse and your possessions,
the British Museum is full of obsessions that you have with us.

You set the standard in which we will never come close,
so I don't blame the perming agenda for what it promotes, because black
mothers simply do not have the time to maintain their daughter's.

Do you know what it feels like for a child not to play with you because
you're coloured?
If they can say that in the open, what do they say behind closed doors?
What that our men are thugs and our women are whores?
It's taught not embedded.
Never forget where your head is.

It's now shoved against the wall because I fit the description of a suspect.
Standard procedure.
Or are you just eager to torment another black child because you think
he has large amounts of weed?
Is that aloud?

All for your conclusion to be, nothing is found on said persons, you're all the same just different versions.

A teacher once demanded that me and my friends turned off the music because it was inappropriate,
But there was no swearing or explicit content yet she just assumed there was.
These are the same teachers to be about protesting for global warming, veganism or political rights, but when it came to Black lives matter not a single teacher was insight, because our plight is for us to deal with.

Why does the word black make you more and uncomfortable than racism itself?

I was robbed of my childhood. My Mum once told me to never run for a bus, because you always attract the wrong attention.
But it doesn't matter if I run, stand, or dance, you don't see how clean my heart is it just see me as a target.

FIRST IMPRESSIONS

By Ogochukwu Madu

Your eyes graze over,
Vowels and consonants blend.
You assume I'm a foreigner.
Foe, and not friend

Your eyes glance over,
Deep skin, melanated.
You assume I'm loud.
A wild temper, ego inflated.

Your mind presumes my speech,
Thick accent and broken.
Assumes colloquial language
Jargon and slang spoken.

Your mind presumes unintelligence,
The language that I speak.
Mind ponders over my origins
My background is what you seek.

Your mind whispers I'm menacing
The look in my eyes is vile
My nature is malevolent
To deceive and beguile.

So, you've drawn to your conclusion.
First impressions have been set.
But the funny thing is,
I haven't even spoken yet.

GRANDMA'S GARDEN

By Bruna Gushurst-Moore

grandma's garden, bungalowed along the rim
in a pale pine clad,
low slung with siding and cleanable by hose,
skittered up the hill with a sandstone paving leader
next clipped conifer and trimmed lawn,
all edged brown

as neat as 1953 could make neat, post-modern,
and neat still in 1972, as though the heat of the years
could not dent this ordered border of lawn, needle, lawn, needle,
all dry and tall and trim and perfectly in its place

but between the manicure of branch and carefully pruned
pine knee, each length twisted just so, a bonsai of intention,
lay a hint of darkness, a cool gaped under branch, quiet behind
the knotted bark,
black

...

and I wonder now who you pressed to clip
these bits organic into ordered hint
of rightness, subdued out of the light, slight.

Not you, in your pale blue floral dress and pale blue coif,
soft of hand with steel girding.

Grandma - who mowed the grass?

HAIR TO WORK

By Curtis Brown

I admit
        to finding it intriguing-
                the way I choose to wear
my afro hair dictates
                who and how they do, or don't say
                hello,
        in passing me -
nod, cracked by a claiming
                        smile, groomed
                                dodge of familiarity, diverted
                gazes of discreet disgust.
I say, look away
        if you must. Cut your eyes
shorter
        than these jagged curls
                of salt and pepper.
I'll not answer your savage cries
                of uncivil vagabond.
Instead I'll turn my luscious lips
inwards,
        lick away bristly wars
                mongering beneath
                        this dense undergrowth of moustache
        and beard. Maybe
soon enough,
                                I'll clip away rough edges, rejoin
                                topiarised illusions of civilised, cool
                                my flaming crown, to fit the masses
                                        of follicled follies.

Or maybe I'll burn within
          my own bush, just so I can
     start to grow again
          from my forest floor. Whatever…
I choose.

I AM NOT

By Marcus Tickner

(It's dark in this container
and there's not sufficient air-)
*I cannot bear to look at him
or acknowledge that he's here!*

*Cut off his thing and tie him up,
sew his lips and shut him up,
then post him back to sender
and ignore that he was born.*

*Documents in dusty vaults -
record the crimes they've done-*
(But I'm not the cause of others' faults
or the inventor of the gun!)

*-Yes, a shame about his gender,
but the one he chose is wrong…
just post him back to sender
and ignore that he was born.*

*They've opinions and they're troublesome,
they differ from ourselves -
for now we'll mark him* **THIS WAY UP,**
*and keep him on the shelf.
And when the postal worker comes,
his box can be withdrawn.
Then we'll post him back to sender
and ignore that he was born.*

MOTHER SAID DO IT 10X BETTER

By Esther Odufuwa

Mother said do it ten times better even if it is to read a book,
It doesn't matter what you learn only, how you look.
She said being a person of colour in a white land,
Is something many people can never truly understand
Being denied a chance because of the colour of your skin
Shows how hard it is to actually ever win.

Mother said do it ten times better so they can't have anything to say
Whether it's the way you dress or even how you play
Being told this morning after morning right before school
Really made me question those who were put in rule
Why was my success considered a mistake?
And why did the way I act either make or break?

Mother said an 8 wasn't enough why couldn't I get a 10
She said an 8 wasn't good enough in front of white men
Mother repeated being black was perfection nothing below
Because in this land they will always try to hide your glow

Our uniqueness is considered strange
And no matter how much we fight, the system will never change
Being black in this land is a struggle everyday
But it's something we must do to make our rights stay

Mother told me I should always come first
Because as I grow it would definitely become worst
I have been hearing 'do it better' since the day of my birth
Because mother said it was the only way I could find my place
on this earth

So I did ten times better all the time
Because if I didn't I would never make a dime
I never settled for less and always aimed high
Even if the racism brought tears to my eyes

It pained me to see that mother was right
That in order to reach success I had to fight
Harder than anyone else for that job offer
Because I had to do it ten times better.

MY TOWER OF SMALL STICKS

By Abdi-Aziz Suleiman

When I did well at school with the sweetest smile my mum gave me
a stick.
My aunt in return for freshly cut grass and a well arranged garden
gave me another.
My friend's mum asked me to carry her shopping but in return
she gave me two.
My father's stories filled my pockets with so many sticks
I could barely walk.

Each day I took those sticks and placed them carefully in my room.
I washed, marked and put them on top of each other.
Slowly, carefully, lovingly the tower of my self grew till one day
a racist man, on a random street threw his words at me and I went home
to see my tower of small sticks shattered.

OPPRESSION

By Barbara Campbell

It feels like a downer
But don't let that familial feeling get you down
Rise like the phoenix from the ashes

Power is an almighty persuader
You are made to feel out of place
Get back in line, I am the boss
Don't dare question my integrity

The game is this
You do as I say
We never gone a be equals
Not on my watch, that's the rules

Who are you to cry victim?
When you are the perpetrator
Back to the tricks of ol' Massa and slave
Just scratch the surface
What do we bleed?

Disrespect runs through the veins
Pumping hatred to the heart
Perspiration stinks of contempt
For your fellow man

This ideology of race and class
Disparity because of the colour of your skin
Permeates through every stratum of our society
The threat of the other

Trying to work out what's the paranoia
I am sure of who I am
Standing strong up against opposition
I will always speak out
Remaining strong
Oppress me not
Not on my watch

OUR STREET

By Santhilea Yung

The parents said our kind don't mix
I didn't think it could be fixed
My daughter didn't make a fuss
When they told her, "You can't play with us"

Her friendly smiles seared my incredulous heart
Her cheerful greetings became an art
When her enemies found hate over-spills
One thing left in the cup was my daughter's good-will

Now, they share their lives and homes
Friendships have blossomed and enormously grown
My daughter defined herself as free
To show her colours beautifully

The bloody battle for justice has begun
But on Our Street, it's patience that won
From a child with magic that's true
The parents have learned something new.

I'm glad she didn't want to hear
A parent's childhood pain and fear
"It's about the love", my daughter says
It made us all change our ways.

RACISM

By Josephine Santamaria Yung

Racism is like potato soup

Absolutely disgusting

Cannot stand it

It feels like pain in your stomach

Sizzling hot boiling water in my head!

More than unfair

RACISM IS REAL BUT THE JOURNEY CONTINUES

By Deanne Heron

I hold tight precious memories of my uncle chatting cheerfully, watching my sad, frightened face in his rear view mirror,

Left by my ambitious mother who was 'sent for', Uncle drove me to the airport with Aunty hugging and reassuring me to reduce my terror.

Nine years old, I boarded the spaceship-like BOAC aeroplane, dressed in lovingly made 1960s smart blue suit with matching gloves and hat,

Aunty's final words echoed in my head and for many years gave me strength, "Always do your best, Baby. No more crying, you're better than that."

Still frightened but curious now, I was escorted with a group of white American children by a stewardess from hot sunshine onto air-conditioned freezing plane,

As the aeroplane took off, shivering, I looked out of the window at my beautiful, hot island, wondering if I would ever see it or my family again.

No smiles or welcome from any of the other children who looked me up and down while whispering to each other,

Eyes wide open, looking up and down, around and around, there were too many things assaulting my five senses for me to bother.

I loved their musical, lilting accents which made me in embarrassment keep my patois accent quiet as I attentively listened,

To my mother's amusement, I was speaking like an American, not a Jamaican by the time, next day, I arrived in busy Britain.

At the airport I saw adults rushing like frightened ants, I discovered fog and snow, smoking chimneys, thinking too that the houses were on fire,

Paraffin heaters, blazing coal fires, the rag and bone man collecting used goods on his cart with bobbing balloons; I was quickly immersed in the racist mire.

On my first day at primary school, the only black in the village, the 'N' word was spat at me by other children with sly punches and kicks in hateful spite,

I didn't understand what it meant or the reason for monkey noises and being told to go back to the jungle, I just knew something wasn't right.

I knew well, mango groves with delicious sweet golden fruit, pineapples, yam and bananas growing in acres of organic land,

I also knew woods and the lush green Blue Mountains but returning to the jungle in Africa, I couldn't until I was much older understand.

To fit in I had to lose my strong patois accent overnight and from a young age develop a steel backbone to be my best and cope,

Confused, I climbed the steep education ladder to make Aunty and Granny in heaven proud of my determination and hope.

"Don't take any notice of them for they don't know any better," my mother said when I often came home from school in tears with bruises and bites,

Targeted by bullies, I was punished by teachers who couldn't see the woods from the trees, believing the lies that I was aggressive and had started the fights.

Coming to cold Britain, for the first time I saw my beautiful difference as a negative thing and for many years it made me withdrawn and shy,

As I got older and rediscovered my worth, I threw out self-doubt and racism made me determine to be my best and not in frustration ask why, why, why?

It deeply damages psychologically when in public you know most people look at you slyly saying negative things behind your back,

When you look at them with a friendly smile or greeting, they mumble under their breath, quickly walk away without even making eye contact.

Watched suspiciously or ignored in shops, my change thrown down onto the counter, even when I was the first in the queue but last to be served,

My ancestors shed blood, lost lives in many wars, came on ships and aeroplanes to help rebuild Britain, so is this really what today we deserve?

I'm glad I had the courage to aim high for the peak of the mountain, be the best that I can be and ensure my children do the same,

Now, grey haired and smiling in satisfaction, covering my deep scars in soothing educational balm, I share survival skills to beat racists at their destructive games.

Going into schools and colleges for Black History Month, I teach true, colourless history to children, regardless of ethnicity,

So we all know ourselves and the sacrifices many people in the commonwealth made to protect and to rebuild Britain, our so called *'Mother Country'*.

RUBY – EVERYONE IS EQUAL UNDER THE LAW

By Jim McRobert

It was in 1954 that the Law was passed;
Education to be equal in every class
Six years to conform in every State
ignoring arguments and folks of hate
New Orleans was a city where God was White
people of shade were not there by right
Anyone of Colour was classed as Slave
to act against one had to be brave

Desegregation of children; Black or White
one school for all would never be right
One of two schools was handed this task
William Frantz Elementary had to lose its mask
but the School set a Test to trick any child
since Blacks were stinking and so reviled

Her parents whispered what will we do
She has the right ain't this a stew
This Mother was strong; she said 'Yes'
Our daughter should go she passed their Test

Little Ruby Bridges was six and sweet
keen for school just down the street
innocent in life She did not know
that people demanded she did not go
She had Police protection each day in line
Government Marshals thro' rain and shine
in an empty class with only one teacher
who defied the crowd; was there to meet her

Threats were made to this little girl
each one she ignored with an iron will
if given the chance they'd feed her poison
drinking water or what her lunch be on

To get into William Frantz I had to sit a Test
and Mama says I must do my best
answer the questions every one
and I know I'll pass cause it's a lot of fun
I'll miss my pals when I'm at this school
Learnin' so important that's Mama's rule
I know my numbers from one to a hundred
an' all about Presidents livin' an' dead.

You know two men in suits came to our door
to escort me to school; I don't know what for
I was taken off in a big shiny car
Dad said five blocks; that's not very far
It was like Mardi Gras with crowds in the street
an' I was so excited at who I should meet
There was folks yellin', some celebration
for My day at school, My ordination?

I went up the steps and into the school
there was no one there, it wasn't so cool
No one. No teachers, an' vacant
so I sat at a desk; wrote a note to my Aunt

I told Mama an' Da there was no one there
Should I go back? It wasn't fair
but I had to go with the men in the suits
I kissed Mama, I had no excuse

The crowds were there yelling at me
with Policemen an' fightin' to get free
an I felt real scared but I didn't let on
once inside the school the feeling had gone
There in a room I met Mrs Hendry a teacher
who grinned an' clapped the moment she saw me

Yes, as soon as I saw her I would be her Teacher
a wonderful girl with an alluring feature
each day, each week, for a whole long year
I taught Ruby with never a tear
every day I addressed her in our Class
in every Subject from PE to Maths
We sang, we played; time passed us by
slowly children came back; we didn't ask why

Da lost his job, Mama banned from the store
Grandpa's land, he doesn't have any more
I had bad dreams an' a psychologist came
who then brought his wife, she made it a game
an' friends an' neighbours gathered round
Da got a job, it made me real proud
an' my Teacher Mrs Hendry she got the sack
but I promised her then I'd never look back

"For one whole year we escorted that kid
each day she would grin an' did what was bid
what courage in that child as she stood in the crowd
if she'd been my daughter, boy I'd be proud
If I had any thoughts about Black or White
what we gained from that girl was to stand for what is Right"

Quote from the US Marshalls.

SAFE PLACES

By Christiana Aliu

Some people make you feel
like home, after a long flight with those
who made you feel
not quite the right fit for the first-class cabin.

Some people make you feel like home, and
welcome you with warm peach cobblers
whose sweet juice runs down your chin, as
you burst with the loud laughter
of self-conscious-less.

You fall asleep with both eyes
closed, and lips wide open
with unfinished

speech. They'll remember where the conversation
chipped in the morning, as you share a pot
of coffee that never stings too hot. Some people

make you feel like home,
through life's journey. Like warm beds that
work their midnight magic; you
wake up ready to board that flight again
even though, the seats
still don't fit right.

(For Arlette, Babs, Catherine, Daniel, Fiona and Keith)

STRANGE FRUIT

By Lorna Callery-Sithole

*'On a scale of 1-10
how black is your husband?'*

He is black

Black as riverbed rocks
orchard shadows
an ebony lake

Black as bass notes
of music played
during midnight serenades

Black as sooty lashes
an evening coat
grit on the road

Black as deep-sea echoes
sheer shadows
on crests of waves

Black as interstellar
of *Whoosh!* whispered softly
black as my pleasure

Black as midnight
the pupil of your iris
storm clouds overhead

Black as alchemist's fire
transforming dark matter into gold
that sits at the ends of rainbows

Black as the panther
who fought for freedom
when black was something other

Black as creation
Black as your ancestors
Black as perfection

Black as a black hole
to another dimension
where black is white
and white is black

THE BLACK C.V. SUMMARY

By Shara Lewis-Campbell

PERSONAL STATEMENT
Andelea is Swahili, but I'll accept Andrew for workplace purposes
Email changes from time to time
HR doesn't comprehend Afrikaans
When you phone me ask for nappy-headed nigg-er

CAREER OBJECTIVE:
Well-versed in labor duties for various organisations
for over forty years.

CAREER SUMMARY:
Ushered & taught workers to submit to Master's by effectively
performing tap dances on desks with heavy boots, while
White colleagues blacken their faces for regional management.
Use defaming techniques against People of Color to receive
compliments: subordinates should forget their mental &
physical pain, speak plain English to heal & produce Negros for
a top quality workplace.

WORK EXPERIENCE/DUTIES:
Not able to perch due to unrest,
I am whatever you see,
I work for relief.

I believe I was hired to sleep in graves
coping with ghosts of my ancestor's labor
as I slave-drive for white saviors.

I continue to work hoping to grieve
off sweaty tears that perspires from
adrenaline & blood.

I read reports when I'm told,
I write memos with white hands,
my voice is dead.

I would pull strings, but I'm only a source of ventriloquism.

THE GHOST WALKERS

By Christiana Aliu

We walk beside others unseen, unfelt, un-
discovered. We meander through the cities
and make a living by being ghost walkers. We smile but
no one smiles back, we are but the passing breeze that slices
through blank skin. They look away and pull their jackets
closer. Prejudice is a devious wind to navigate.

The economy is built by the likes of us. Those who lay
the bricks, but are never present
for the grand openings. Who falter
and fail for others to rise and step on our heads, as they climb
on the ladder held by our hands.

We sit in classrooms, in ghostly silence as we watch
others speak with words we do not comprehend. In a
language that is second and not first nature to us. We are
grateful no one is aware we occupy the empty spaces. Our
embarrassment is only known to us. We leave feeling
more uneducated than we arrived. Emptied of all we thought
we knew. A shell of who we once were.

THE GRIND

By Stuart Lodge

I sit there,
The target of your abuse,
Your lies,

You preach that we are the same,
That we are one,
And you enforce your social apartheid,

We live together,
But are a million miles apart,
Separated by our otherness,

Statements of your lack of racism,
Are hollow,
When you ask me to abandon who I am.

TINTS AND SHADES

By Lorna Callery-Sithole

do you remember
mixing two colours
to create a whole new colour?

it's just like that
you are the new colour
you are perfection

you are

copper pearl
warm cinnamon
caramel kisses

you are

puddle jumper
gritty woodpigeon
secret mission

you are

heart of jungle
thundercloud and zephyr
paradise found

you are

cuddle bug
hinkypunk
dancing water

you are

electro chill
singin the blues
stardust highway

you are

misty dreams
punctuating
shallow skies

you are

tigress
rock solid
against glass ceilings

you are

poetry in motion
a cappella
dream weaver

you are

bear hugs
thick as thieves
an unfound door

you are

soft panther
grey shingle
dance of goddesses

you are

TO THE YOUNG PEOPLE OF COLOUR

By Cara Dixon-Napier

To the young people of colour,
Are you aware that your skin means more than your words?

When will we be we?
Extremities for queen and country,
I've become the acceptable minority for equality.
I am Less than, for them.
Always available for cultural education,
because one black female has all the information?
When will we be we?

For every award that you gain,
every ladder they Let you climb,
every success that you achieve,
Invite a million ignorant eyes;
waiting, hoping, cursing, for the "ethnic" to leave.
Questioning whether it's your talent and skill?
Or a minority quota, agenda to fill?

Extremities for queen and country,
I've become the acceptable minority for equality.
I am Less than, for them.

You must always disassemble your culture in public.
Pick a piece, a part to show,
diminish your fire to embers.
Appealing to majority is the work of minority.
Euro centric beauty standards,
Alluring "exotic" appropriation accepted.

The stolen appropriation adorned by black women rejected.
The constant Anticipated Aggression of a Black Female spirit,
Not true, not acceptable.
Yet ever so completely, believable.
You must conform to confirm
To create opportunities achievable.
Whisper to prosper
British before black
You feel it from birth, the target aimed right on

Conform to confirm
Conform to confirm

British before black
The target will always be aimed at

Engrained intuition coexists in your brain.
From your first realisation of indifference.
Emits eager pride of cultural identity,
Blown out in an instant,
irreparable playground scars of cultural shame.
never spoken, understood.
a sixth sense,
Is this atmosphere dangerous?
Am I diluted enough to stay here and be safe?
when to be,
how to be,
Enough of me?
The acceptable, approachable, ambient version of me.
How to talk without talking?
when to walk but not run?
How to hide success in the shade, not to shine too bright in
their sun.

Are you aware your skin means more than your words?
The shade, hue, freckles and scars a heavier weight?
I'm 3rd generation and still I'm afraid.
A culture disassembled, reassembled;
before the public eye
Swallowed, your voice,
Ignored, your thoughts,
But when its needed,
how they weaponise our cry.

UNDERLYING CONDITIONS

By Barbara Campbell

Pandemic Virus – causations
Poor health, underlying conditions
Socio-economic injustices worldwide
We the BAME are bottom of the pile

Striving to elevate society's stratifications
Unacknowledged by the glass ceiling barriers
Standing in the way of our success
We Care Workers unselfishly standing on the frontline
Innocently giving up our lives for the cause
No protection from the unseen beast lurking
Ready to take our lives in the thousands

I was such a man faithful and devoted to my family
I was strong but made weak by an underlying condition
Taken too soon by the wretched virus
Who will be taking care of my wife and children?
Now I am gone

Innate narratives borne out of the past slave mentality
Covert but alive and kicking, in motion
Now permeating through the consciousness of a different
generation
Rising out of a heinous crime
Against a Black man, a black population
Ricochet – rebounding across nations

We must not forget
This punishment did not fit the crime
Unity is our mantra; we are all shouting out loud
Revolting against all the odds – **BLACK LIVES MATTER**

WHAT YOU SAYING

By Dhruti Shah

You can't read English
Yet you're referenced in academic texts
You look so exotic
Yet they think you brown women are the same
You sound too ethnic
Yet it's a London accent so British
You smell of curry
Yet they want the recipe for their homes
You must speak Hindi
So an assumption of my culture yeah?
That monobrow must go
But you like the art of Frida Kahlo?
You can stay junior
So promotion is for certain types
Microaggressions
You understand the double talk that happens
Some are explicit
Others more underhand with what they say
But peel away layers
You hear it all even if nothing is said.

YOU DON'T EVEN KNOW ME – WHAT'S IN A NAME?

By Poetry Girl 2.0

I've worked with you for years, but yet, you call me Mary, when my name
is Jane…

Hmmm, if my skin was like yours, would your brain fit in my face
as well as my name?

Mary is the black lady in Finance, how clichéd, I'm Jane.
We don't even look the same!

Yes, we are both black and yes, we're both women, but
Mary's the thin one, I'm fatter, I'm JANE!

Yes, we are both women, and yes, we're both black, but
Mary wears contacts and I wear different shades
of designer glasses in the main…

Yes, we are so different, that we are the same…

Tomorrow, I'll call you Peter, or maybe even Jack…

I've seen both of them, and neither of them is bald nor fat…

SECTION 5:

About Black in White

ABOUT BLACK IN WHITE

Black in White was established in late 2020 following the publication of an eponymous book of poems that I wrote about some of my experiences of racism in the workplace. I was motivated to write the poems following the murder of George Floyd in May 2020. Like so many of us, I was deeply struck by how entrenched and endemic racist attitudes continue to result in such horrifying killings and the daily demeaning of black people. I reflected on my own experiences of racism – particularly while working in the corporate world where such things are rarely spoken about – and decided to tell some of my stories. And so *Black in White* was born.

Our Mission

Our mission is to contribute to the conversation around ending racism by:

- ❖ Creating enlightening products including poetry books and discussion guides

- ❖ Running engaging events including book launches and poetry readings; and

- ❖ Providing educational services including equality, diversity and inclusion consultancy and mentoring

Where to Purchase

The *Black in White* poetry books (in paperback and Kindle formats) are available to purchase from major online book retailers, including Amazon, Barnes & Nobles and Waterstones. They can also be ordered, together with our discussion guides, poem posters, poem postcards and other products, from our online store: **www.blackinwhiteservices.co.uk/store**.

The Black in White team

The team comprises the following amazing individuals who work with me and play a key role in helping to plan and implement all of the *Black in White* activities and initiatives:

Get in touch

We'd love to hear from you if you are looking for a creative and engaging way to have conversations about racism in your workplace, in an educational setting and beyond; to access our equality, diversity and inclusion consultancy or mentoring services; or to ask about bespoke projects.

Contact Charlotte at **charlotte@blackinwhiteservices.co.uk**

www.blackinwhiteservices.co.uk

Follow us on **Instagram and Twitter: @Blackinwhite27**
and on **LinkedIn: Black in White Ltd**

Subscribe and like our **YouTube channel: Charlotte Shyllon**

"In work, in life, in everything, kick racism out, respect is king."

9 781787 920248